New Zealand Travel Guide

Exploring Incredible Landscapes

Disclaimer and Copyright Notice

© Copyright 2022 by booksclub.org - All rights reserved.

Please note that the information contained herein is for educational purposes. Every effort has been made to ensure precision, timeliness, and reliability. There are no explicit or implied guarantees of any kind.

Readers accept that the author does not commit to making law, political, job guidance, or a quick rich scheme. By reading this notice, the reader agrees that we are not responsible under any circumstances for any direct or indirect losses incurred as a result of using the information found in this text, including- but not just errors, omissions, or inaccuracies. This book is protected by copyright. That is for private use only. You should not use, alter, distribute, offer, quote, or paraphrase some of the content. Neither author nor copyright owner has consented to anyone to copy it.

When this is violated, legal action can be taken.

<u>Table of Contents</u>

Introduction

If you're looking for a fantastic travel destination with something for everyone, look no further than New Zealand. This small country is packed with incredible scenery, from metropolitan cities to rolling hills and trails, surf breaks and wine country, glaciers, and treks. And of course, the friendly locals are always happy to help make your visit even more enjoyable.

No matter your interests, you'll find plenty to do in New Zealand. So start planning your trip today and get ready for an unforgettable adventure!

New Zealand is a country with a rich history and culture. The people of New Zealand are known for their friendly and welcoming nature, and many traditions and national symbols make New Zealand unique. The country is also home to stunning scenery, including mountains, forests, and beaches. Whether you're visiting for business or pleasure, I hope you enjoy your time in New Zealand. Welcome!

Chapter 1: Welcome to New Zealand

Southeast of Australia in the Pacific Ocean is the island nation of New Zealand. It is divided into the North and South Islands. In the Maori language, New Zealand is called Aotearoa, meaning "land of the long white cloud." Abel Tasman first discovered New Zealand in 1642, but it was not until 1769, thanks to James Cook, that this country was known about. The inhabitants of New Zealand are called Kiwi after the bird of the same name, which is the national symbol of this country. During the day, it is buried in the ground, and at night it comes out searching for food. It can be seen in the reserve where it lives in special conditions. Devastating earthquakes and constant volcanic activity are frequent in this area. New Zealand has about 4.5 million inhabitants, and this area is one of the most sparsely populated areas in the world.

Along with the beautiful nature in New Zealand, adrenaline sports, especially Bungee jumping, are a unique attraction for tourists. You will get the impression that you have come to the end of the world. Although New Zealand is a desirable country to live in, it is a country of beautiful nature, national parks, and high standards. Young people here suffer from the "end of the world"

complex, so they want to find work in Australia and Great Britain.

<u>New Zealand at a glance</u>

Capital: Wellington, 370,000 inhabitants

Currency: New Zealand dollar (approx. €0.50)

Food: seafood, Kiwi

Attractions: Bay of Islands; warm mud, geysers, Maori culture near Rotorua; Waitomo Caves; Tongariro National Park; fjords and glaciers on the South Island; skiing in Queenstown; whale watching in Kaikoura.

Population: 4.43 million

Languages: English, Maori

<u>Geography and climate</u>

The numerous islands of New Zealand have varied climates. The majority of the nation has heavy rainfall and warm temperatures. However, it can get very chilly in the highlands. The main parts of the country are the North Island and the South Island, separated by the Cook Strait. The 44,281 square meters of North Island comprises low, volcanic mountains. The North Island has hot springs and geysers due to its volcanic past. The Southern Alps, a glacier-covered mountain range running northeast to southwest, is located on the 58,093 square kilometers of South Island. Mount Cook, also known as Aoraki in Maori, is the mountain's highest point. The island comprises the pristine Canterbury plains to the east of those mountains. The island's southwest shore is rocky with fjords and densely forested. Fiordland, New Zealand's largest national park, is also located in this region.

<u>Biodiversity</u>

One of the most important features to note about New Zealand is its high level of biodiversity. Since most of its species are endemic (i.e., only on the islands), the country is considered biodiverse. This led to the development of environmental awareness in the country and ecotourism.

1.1 New Zealand now and then – a brief history lesson

Dutch adventurer Abel Tasman made the first European discovery of New Zealand in 1642. With his illustrations of the northern and southern islands, he was also the first to try to map the islands. Captain James Cook arrived at the islands in 1769 and established the first European presence there. He also started a run of three South Pacific excursions, during which he carefully examined the coastline. Europeans settled formally in New Zealand in the late 18th and early 19th centuries. These settlements included some hunts for timber, seals, and whales. It was not until Great Britain occupied the islands in 1840 that the first autonomous European colony was founded.

As a result, there were numerous wars between the British and the local Maori. The Treaty of Waitangi, which both parties signed on February 6, 1840, guaranteed the protection of Maori lands in exchange for the tribes' acceptance of British rule. Shortly after this agreement was signed, the British attack on Maori land continued. The wars between the Maori and the British grew during the 1860s with the Maori Wars. Before those wars, the constitutional government began to develop during the 1850s. Maori were given reserved seats in the newly formed parliament in 1867.

The parliamentary system of government was firmly entrenched by the late 19th century. In 1893, women were granted the right to vote. Today, New Zealand is regarded as an autonomous member of the Commonwealth of Nations and has a parliamentary system of government. It was legally proclaimed to have power in 1907 and lacks a clear written constitution.

1.2 Seven reasons to visit New Zealand

1. Unspoiled and diverse landscape

New Zealand is known for its magical landscape, which includes vast mountain ranges, lush rainforests, and large volcanoes.

Indeed, few areas can compete with New Zealand's natural beauty. Precisely because of this, it is no wonder that this country has become so sought after as a film location. Numerous movies, including The Lord of the Rings and The Chronicles of Narnia, were filmed here. Take a risk and, like Bilbo Baggins, explore a place of unspoiled beauty!

2. Adrenaline activities

Another popular name for New Zealand is the "adventure capital of the world." In it, you will find unique and most exciting adrenaline activities. Explore natural tunnels and caves and get to know flora and fauna. In addition, try some exciting activities such as ziplining, rafting, rock climbing, zorbing, and more. Considering that New Zealand and adrenaline go hand in hand, this place is a must for all adventurers.

3. The unique world of wildlife

New Zealand is best known for the kiwi bird, the national symbol, but the unique animal species in this area do not end there. New Zealand is hugely well known as a paradise for animal lovers. Here you can hear different birds, swim with dolphins, ride horses or watch whales or birds. Several endangered species are also found here, such as the yellow-eyed penguin, the kea parrot, and Hector's dolphin, the smallest and rarest dolphin species worldwide.

4. Maori culture

The inhabitants of New Zealand are popularly called Kiwis. Still, they are people with expressed pride in their rich history and traditions. Maori stories and legends were passed down from generation to generation and told about the creation of the island. Legend has it that the brash demigod Maui raised New Zealand from the sea with his magic hook. If you want to hear more stories about the dynamic Moorish history, visit Mount Hikurangi with a local guide.

5. The Maori language

One of New Zealand's three official languages is Maori, which locals use to express their identity and culture. Until the 19th century, the language did not exist in written form, but Maori communicated with symbols. You can try to learn Maori with the Ngapuhi tribe for a fun, interactive experience as part of Taiamai Tours Heritage Journeys. Visitors here can learn much about the Maori way of life, language, spirituality, and traditions. All in all, a great experience will reveal to you all what makes New Zealand unique.

6. Food

The kitchen is based on traditional Maori dishes with a touch of British and Mediterranean cuisine. Most dishes are made from local products. One of the favorite foods is freshwater crab, which is considered a delicacy. Another famous dish is savory pies, made with different fillings such as minced meat, cheese, and fish. Sweet tooth lovers must try the popular pavlova dessert, which is made from egg whites, whipped cream, and fresh fruit. In addition, you should try the hokey pokey made from vanilla ice cream and pieces of caramel.

7. National Parks

New Zealand boasts 13 beautiful national parks that cover ⅓ of the country. You can see numerous mountain peaks and sparkling lakes through spacious, protected areas. The wilderness of the national parks is mostly untouched and allows you to look back 1000 years. Among these parks, one holds the title of the cleanest lake in the world – Lake Nelson National Park. The blue lake has visibility up to 80 meters deep, which makes it an almost magical crystal lake.

1.3 Must-see attractions

1. Fiordland National Park and Milford Sound

Fiordland National Park, a World Heritage Site, guards some of the most breathtaking scenery in the nation. This stunning environment, which includes the well-known fjords of Milford, Dark, and Doubtful Sounds, was formed by glaciers. Here, visitors can explore forest cascades, open-air islets, rainbow rainforests, rainforests, lakes, and rugged mountain peaks. Unsurprisingly, the park is a haven for hikers with some of the best walks in the country, including the famous Milford Track, Sea kayaking is a popular way to explore the fjords, and visitors can enjoy a scenic flight over the park for a bird's eye view of the stunning beauty.

2. Bay of Islands, North Island

The stunning Bay of Islands can be reached by car from Auckland in three hours. It is a sailing sanctuary with more than 144 islets offering a sparkling bay. These warm waters are home to penguins, dolphins, whales, and marlin, and the area is a well-liked location for sport fishing. Sea kayaking along the coast, hiking the island's various paths, relaxing in isolated coves, touring Cape Brett and the well-known Hole in the Rock rock formation, and exploring subtropical woods home to Kauri trees are all enjoyable activities for visitors. Star towns in the area such as Russell, Opua, Paihia, and Kerikeri are excellent bases for exploring this beautiful bay.

3. Queenstown, South Island

The adventure capital of New Zealand and one of the top tourist sites in the nation, Queenstown is tucked between the dazzling Lake Wakatipu's shoreline and the snow-capped Remarkables. Bungee jumping, jet boating, white-water rafting, paragliding, rock climbing, mountain biking, and downhill skiing are just a few heart-pounding activities.

An excellent network of hiking paths also allows visitors to explore the breathtaking alpine environment. Adventure sports aside, Queenstown offers all the creature comforts with first-class hotels, spas, restaurants, galleries, and shops. It is also an excellent base for trips to Central Otago, where visitors can explore the gold mining towns and scenery of Middle Earth from the famous Lord of the Rings films.

4. North Island's Lake Taupo and Tongariro National Park

National Park, in the heart of the North Island and a short distance from Lake Taupo, New Zealand's largest lake, is a dual World Heritage Site for its outstanding volcanic characteristics and significance to Maori culture. To protect this holy area, Maori Chief Te Heuheu Tukino IV gave the people of New Zealand the volcanic peaks of Tongariro, Ngauruhoe, and a portion of Ruapehu in 1887. An area of stunning beauty with towering volcanoes, turquoise lakes, dry plateaus, alpine meadows, and hot springs, Tongariro is one of the oldest national parks in the world.

6. Fox and Franz Josef Glaciers, South Island

Among the most popular glaciers in the world, Franz Josef and Fox glaciers are the main tourist attractions in the spectacular Westland Tai Poutini National Park. Both rivers flow from some of the highest peaks of the Southern Alps to the nearby sea, where mild coastal conditions make it easy for visitors to explore them on foot. Guided walks lead to the twisted frozen landscape of ice caves and peaks at the glacier's base. Visitors are taken to the top of these enormous tongues of ice via seaplanes and helicopters for an airborne look.

7. Abel Tasman National Park and the Split Stone

Split Apple Rock, or the split stone in the Abel Tasman National Park on the South Island, is another wonder of nature. This geological rock formation in the shape of a halved apple is one of New Zealand's most photographed motifs.

It can be reached in several ways, and a favorite among tourists is by kayak. Seaplanes and helicopters take tourists to the top of these enormous tongues of ice for an airborne look. If you like camping, this is one of the best places for it. Only hammocks are not allowed.

8. Aoraki National Park / Mount Cook, South Island

The tallest peaks in New Zealand rise above the alpine landscapes of Aoraki National Park, also known as Mount Cook National Park, in the heart of the Southern Alps. It is one of the best places to hike since it is home to the Tasman Glacier, the longest glacier in the world, and Mount Cook, the tallest mountain in the country. More than 40% of the park is covered in glaciers. Sir Edmund Hillary trained here in preparation for his illustrious ascent of Mount Everest. With over 300 alpine plants and 40 bird species varieties, nature lovers will enjoy the variety of flora and animals. Mount Cook Village is a great starting point for visiting the park and planning activities like scenic flights, ski tourism, heli-skiing, hunting, hiking, and excursion tours.

9. Auckland, North Island

Blessed with two sparkling harbors, Auckland, the "City of Sails," is the largest city in New Zealand and the most numerous Polynesian city in the world. The town is surrounded by beaches with white and black sand, hiking paths through forests, gorgeous coves, islands, and volcanoes, making it the ideal starting point for day trips and outdoor experiences.

Visitors can scale the 328m Sky Tower to appreciate Auckland's incredible location for spectacular views across the city and hinterland. Auckland is also home to fine dining, a vibrant arts scene, and a revitalized waterfront district packed with boutiques and restaurants.

10. Kaikoura, South Island

Birds, wildlife enthusiasts, and seafood lovers love the charming seaside town of Kaikoura. Tucked between the Seaward Kaikoura Range and the Pacific Ocean, Kaikoura offers excellent coastal walks and popular whale-watching tours. In addition to sperm whales and whales, travelers can spot fur seals, dolphins, and a wide variety of birds, including graceful albatrosses. Kaikoura is known for its freshly caught crab, shellfish, and other seafood.

11. Hobbiton

There are many locations in New Zealand where the Lord of the Rings films were shot, but none of them will take you to Middle Earth as Hobbiton will.

The Shire's beautiful, rolling hills can be found on the Hobbiton Movie Set, where you may explore Hobbit Holes and have a drink at the Green Dragon Inn.

Only on a guided walking tour is it possible to visit Hobbiton, but it's a lot of fun, and you learn a lot about how the movies were made.

12. Lake Pukaki

Lake Pukaki is the largest of the three mountain lakes of New Zealand's Southern Alps on the South Island. This blue jewel is another iconic place, known, among other things, as the location Peter Jackson chose for the hobbit town "Lake Town."

13. Te Whanganui-A-Hei

Cathedral Bay (Cathedral Cove) is a nature reserve on the Coromandel Peninsula and extends over 840 hectares. About 150,000 tourists visit it annually. From the beautiful Hahei Beach, you can walk to Cathedral Cove, where you will see one of the most photogenic scenes on the peninsula.

14. Lonely tree - Wanaka Tree

A lonely willow in the middle of the lake is known as "That Wanaka Tree" or #thatwanakatree. It is a trendy motif on social networks. Quite a few people climb the tree for the best possible photos and damage it. Therefore, the New Zealand authorities have decided to ban such activities in the future. The tree is located in the town of Wanaka on the South Island, an hour's drive from Queenstown.

15. Volcano on White Island

Whakaari / White Island is an active volcano 48 km from the east coast of the North Island in the Bay of Plenty. It has been the most active volcano for 150 thousand years. You can get to the volcano by plane from Whakatane, which will only fly over it, by Frontier Helicopters helicopter, which will also land you on the volcano itself, or by boat on a 90-minute tour. During the flight and boat ride, you will see whales and dolphins in the sea.

16. Moeraki Boulders

Huge round stones on the Moeraki Boulders beach are also quite famous motifs of New Zealand. Located on Koekohe Beach on the Otago Coast between Moeraki and Hampden.

They have existed for 60 million years, and the heaviest among them weighs about 7 tons. The best time to see them in their full beauty is at low tide (when the tide is high, you only see the tops) twice a day, and you can track precisely when that is on the MetService page.

17. Bridal Veil Fall

A beautiful waterfall called Bridal Veil is located on the Pakoka River in the Waikato area. It is 55 meters high, and due to the winds that blow there, you will often see a mist around the waterfall, which is why it looks like a transparent veil. The natives call it Pohono.

18. Pancake Rocks

Rocks that look like stacked pancakes are the most visited tourist attraction on the west coast of New Zealand. The Pancake Rocks in Punakaiki were formed by the sea 30 million years ago and are still being shaped today. Access to the rocks is possible even for people with disabilities.

<u>19. Champagne Pools</u>

Hot-colored springs called champagne pools or Champagne Pools are located in Wai-O-Tap and were created as a result of the eruption of the Tarawera volcano back in 1886. Pink and white terraces splashed with hot water, and a strong sulfur smell attracts tourists searching for unique natural beauty.

1.4 The Language, geography, and climate

English is the dominant language spoken by 98% of the population. The New Zealand variety of English is similar to the Australian type of English, and it is difficult for foreigners to distinguish between the two accents. After World War II, Maori were discouraged from using their language in schools and workplaces, which survived as a community language only in remote areas. Recently, a revitalization process began.

Maori was declared an official language in 1987 and is spoken by 4.1% of the population. Today there are Maori language schools as well as two Maori Television channels. Many places have double names in Maori and English. According to data from the beginning of the 21st century, about 30,000 people (4.2% of the total New Zealand population) speak Maori as their mother tongue daily, and 150,000 occasionally talk and understand it.

After English and Maori, the most widespread is Samoan, followed by French, Hindi, Jue, and Northern Chinese. New Zealand Sign Language is used by about 28,000 people and became an official language in 2006.

<u>Geography and climate</u>

The numerous islands that makeup New Zealand all have varied climates. The majority of the nation has heavy rainfall and warm temperatures. However, it can get very chilly in the highlands. The main parts of the country are the North Island and the South Island, separated by the Cook Strait. Low, volcanic mountains make up the North Island.

The North Island has hot springs and geysers due to its volcanic heritage. The southern island contains the Southern Alps - a mountain massif in a northeast-southwest direction covered by glaciers. Mount Cook, also called Aoraki in Maori, is the mountain's highest point. To the east of those mountains, the island is dry and consists of the pristine Canterbury plains. In the southwest, the island coast is heavily forested and jagged with fjords.

<u>Biodiversity</u>

One of the most important features to note about New Zealand is its high level of biodiversity. Since most of its species are endemic, the country is considered biodiverse. This led to the development of environmental awareness in the country and ecotourism.

<u>What to pack?</u>

1. Sunscreen

2. Trekking boots

3. Camera backpack

4. Travel cards

5. Trekking poles

6. Waterproof rain jacket

7. Head torch

8. Swimsuit/boardies

9. Bug-resistant spray or clothing

10. ID

11. Thermals/layers

12. Beanie

13. Go Pro

14. Portable charger

15. Thick socks

16. Packing cells

17. Insulated jacket

Chapter 2: Tips and tricks

<u>Costs</u>

The general impression is that the prices are a bit more expensive than elsewhere, but even below the average of many European countries. Accommodation can be found at highly reasonable prices, and the food is acceptable enough that you can eat well for the entire duration of your stay. If you eat in a restaurant, it will cost you the same as some mid-range restaurants. As for the payment method, you can pay by card in almost all places.

<u>Internet</u>

Free internet access is not something you will experience as usual here. In most accommodations, the wi-fi signal is very poor or limited to the common area. You are forced to buy a megabyte package for internet access at reception. I recommend purchasing a SIM card from any local operator. Buy one right at the airport.

<u>Rentacar</u>

Transport is the best choice if you want to see as much as possible. Another option is renting a camper, and certainly one of the more popular on the island. Be careful if you decide that you camp in legal places and don't defecate in nature (this goes without saying, but in New Zealand, you could very quickly be fined for this). Public transport is well developed, while buses from various agencies run to most tourist attractions.

2.1 Foods and drinks

Due to historical circumstances, the cuisine of New Zealand was strongly influenced by the culinary tradition of Great Britain for centuries. It was only after 1959 that it slowly but surely began to free itself from its dominance and became open to the cuisines of other cultures, primarily immigrants from all over the world. Therefore, in addition to traditional cuisine and the authentic native Maori cuisine, under the influence of different cuisines from Asia, Oceania, and Europe, there is also a new crossover, i.e., multicultural New Zealand cuisine in New Zealand.

Food comes from the crystal clear sea, rivers, streams, lakes, endless forests, pastures, fertile fields, orchards, and plantations. The most popular meats are lamb and beef. At the same time, different types of poultry and pork are especially represented in the diet of the original New Zealand population, the Maori. As the country is rich in pastures and animal husbandry is very developed, a large part of the lamb and beef on the market comes from free-range farming, so the meat is of exceptional quality and taste. Hunting is highly developed due to the vast forests, so meat dishes of different game types, high and low, are widespread and popular.

New Zealand is especially famous for its high-quality deer meat (deer are also raised on numerous farms), which is exported worldwide. In addition to meat, New Zealand, the leading exporter of meat and dairy products, can also boast of a wealth of different types of freshwater, marine fish, and seafood. New Zealanders can choose from more than eighty different types of fish, including tuna, eels, sardines, and salmon that come to the table from salmon farms and trout that are among the largest in the world.

On the menu are New Zealanders and various shellfish, which in this climate are sometimes twice as big as others, as well as lobsters, crabs, shrimps, and multiple muskrats. Among shellfish, the green-lipped type is trendy. It is sold fresh in otherwise well-stocked supermarkets, and among fish, for example, whitebait and young sardines, only 2 to 4 cm in size, which are a favorite seasonal specialty. Fish and seafood are prepared really differently. They are fried in batter or dried, so dried shellfish, especially oysters, are very popular. Almost all kinds of vegetables and fruits thrive in New Zealand, and avocados, Kiwi, papaya, artichokes, potatoes, and sweet potatoes are very popular in the kitchen.

A particular type of kumara sweet potato and tree tomatoes, called tamarillos, also thrive here. New Zealanders also enjoy various dairy products and thus eat 100 kg of butter and 65 kg of cheese per capita per year, among which are the prized original cheeses, ajhette, and kapiti.

Along with meals, different types of carbonated drinks, wine, and beer are drunk with water, fruit juices, and top-rated fruit wines made from various fruits. A popular drink is lemonade with mineral water, L&P, Lemon&Paeroa, and among the wines New Zealand winegrowers are becoming more and more famous in the world, the white wines: sauvignon blanc and chardonnay and the red: cabernet sauvignon are especially appreciated. New Zealanders are simply crazy about barbecue, especially huge steaks, and are a real barbecue nation.

Moreover, a barbecue is a status symbol of every New Zealand man, so it is inevitably acquired according to the principle that the bigger, the better. Therefore, backyard grills are usually as big as European summer kitchens. Because of the love of grilling, there are places with grills at almost all gas stations and roadside resorts. In addition, New Zealanders also love picnics and family outings in nature. Excursion destinations are equipped with barbecues, firewood, wooden tables, and benches.

<u>BYO restaurant</u>

Depending on the appetite, different small dishes are eaten with the legs between the main meals, the offer of which is vibrant. Under the influence of England, fish and chips and chicken and chips are very popular, fish and chicken with potatoes, which are sold in small diners on almost every corner. Under the influence of America, New Zealanders also enjoy the offer of numerous fast food restaurants, especially their favorite hamburgers. The offer of ready-made meals in extremely well-stocked supermarkets is also prosperous. Supermarkets also have a wide selection of sweets, which New Zealanders also adore. Among the most popular are the traditional "Hokey Pokey" candies and the eponymous vanilla ice cream served with these candies. The list of favorite sweets also includes "Pineapple lumps," pineapple-flavored chocolate candies created in 1935, and "Jaffas" chocolate balls filled with orange. The famous small dishes are dough pillows filled with chopped meat and a particularly original Maori dish, hangi. It is a dish of meat and vegetables, mostly sweet potatoes, prepared traditionally for two to three hours under an earthen oven on hot volcanic stones. New Zealanders like to go to pubs, bars, cafes, and restaurants. Trendy cafes are usually only open from 10 a.m. to 3 p.m. Numerous restaurants, especially in small towns, are primarily small and very simple.

In contrast, the more elite and expensive ones are only found in big cities and tourist centers. As in New Zealand, not all bars have a license to serve alcoholic beverages. Many restaurants operate on the BYO (Bring Your Own) principle. That is, guests, bring their own drinks, which, with a mandatory small tip to the waiter, will be drunk with the meal. Wine and beer are sold in supermarkets. Wine is also bought in specialized wine shops and directly from the winemaker. At the same time, spirits are exclusively offered at unique bottle stores.

2.2 Plan your trip – when to travel

The climate in New Zealand is generally mild, ranging from subtropical in the far north to temperate in the south. Summer lasts from December to February, with temperatures from 21 to 32 ° C, and winter is from June to August, with temperatures from 1 to 15 ° C. And although New Zealand can offer fascinating attractions and activities all year round, this paradise for visitors is best to travel from spring to autumn.

2.3 Where to Stay

Every city in New Zealand has Base Hostels, and the accommodation package costs NZD 250, less than €150. It includes a total of 10 nights in any city with the proviso that one cannot stay more than two nights in one place. This excellent opportunity is also the most popular and cheapest accommodation option to visit as many locations as possible while staying at the end of the world.

2.4 Get Around NZ

<u>By car</u>

If you drive in New Zealand, you will find an excellent network of well-maintained and sealed roads. However, some of them can be rather twisting and narrow depending on the topography, particularly on the North Island. The motorway systems in Auckland, Wellington, Tauranga, and Christchurch make it quite simple to enter and exit the cities; even the travel time is not too bad compared to many other areas in the world. The speed limit is usually 50 km/h (30 mph) in urban areas, with an upper limit of 100 km/h on open roads and motorways. And don't forget to hold left; like in Australia or Great Britain, driving is on the left side of the road. Numerous automobile rental firms exist in airports and other significant locations throughout New Zealand. To receive the greatest deals, booking online is a great idea.

<u>Camper</u>

Over 100,000 motorhomes, often known as campervans locally, travel New Zealand's highways yearly. This is a fairly common way to explore the nation. You can choose from various sizes and configurations depending on your needs and budget. There are basically two options for overnight parking. First, you can make a reservation at a campsite or holiday park. These offers offer places for campervans and, of course, cooking and washing facilities.

Bus

Daily bus services connect most of New Zealand's top destinations, and this is a prevalent transport option for tourists. One of the biggest benefits of taking a bus, aside from the comfort and ease of not having to drive, is the commentary usually provided by the driver. You'll learn more about the locations you pass than you could on your own and are almost guaranteed to pick up a few humorous local jokes!

Tours

An organized training tour is another low-cost and informative transport option in New Zealand. You can choose regional or national tours of various lengths to suit your time frame. Accommodation is usually included, and there can be multiple forms of meals and sightseeing.

Train

Traveling by train is not one of the best ways to get around New Zealand, as the rail network is limited. However, there are several memorable train journeys for tourists; the best is the route between Auckland and Wellington and the TranzAlpin, which crosses the Southern Alps between Christchurch and Greymouth in the south of the island.

Air

New Zealand and JetStar are national carriers operating flights between major hubs and smaller destinations. Competition keeps prices very reasonable, and it's often possible to raise prices at bargain prices. The best way is to book online as much as you can. Smaller operators are also in such specialist destinations as Great Barrier Island and Stewart Island.

Motorbike

It's a fantastic way to see New Zealand, too! A motorcyclist's fantasy is to travel on long, straight highways through a beautiful landscape. Numerous places hire bicycles.

Bicycle

For the intrepid adventurer, cycling can be an attractive option for traveling around New Zealand. Be warned: many steep hills and narrow roads (especially on the North Island) would make cycling dangerous. However, there are other operators across the nation where you may hire a bike or sign up for a tour because so many people visit this location.

Conclusion

Beautiful landscapes have been preserved in their natural magnificence, the sea, mountain peaks and plains, lakes, caves, and active volcanoes. In this contrast of relief features, it looks as if God painted the most beautiful landscapes with a heavenly brush to leave us breathless and placed them on the islands of New Zealand.

Fantastic Maoris are Polynesians who, with their love for nature and coexistence with it, do not leave anyone indifferent but encourage the constant repetition of the sentence: "Oh, Mother Nature!". New Zealand is unique among all nations in many respects. It was one of the last to have people settle there. It is one of the few nations with two national anthems, "God Save The Queen" and "God Defend New Zealand."

Thankyou for Reading!

Please review us and subscribe at

www.booksclub.org